Joanna Kotsoni
Romantic Evening
Fylatos Publishing

This work is copyright. Apart from any use as permitted under the Copyright Act, no part maybe reproduced, copied, scanned, stored in a retrieval system, recorded or transmitted, in any form or by any means, without the prior written permission of the publisher.

Writter: Joanna Kotsoni

© Fylatos Publishing

Contact us at: contact@fylatos.com

Our website : www.fylatos.com

Cover Design: Fylatos Publishing

ISBN: 978-618-80902-8-6

Joanna Kotsoni

Romantic Evening

FYLATOS PUBLISHING

MMXIV

Today

Today a bird passed by a cloud
I wondered what it was
You know, I could not see well
My dreams are all like yellow leaves
Tossed on an empty, sandy shore
Made of gold and silver
Today a nest fell from a tree
I was startled, frightened
You see, I did not know much.
My house was burned by the white frost
Just when everything seemed to be wonderful
It was all lost for no reason
Today my body died upon a photograph
An old one of yours
From then, when we were children
Eros, sighs and your red kisses
Passed before me
And were lost again

Then again

I loved you, yes!
With all the wheat stalks of May
And with all the rest
With all that you hid even deeper than your heart
With all my thoughts when I was far from you
I was jealous, yes!
Then again I never did believe the outside world
I was not dedicated to listening to the words of others
And I admit that it hurt just the same
As if I was seeing a story from the past
Then again, tell me, why are you no longer with me?
Am I, perhaps, to blame for all that?
Did I perhaps, not deserve a little love for a while?
Or did you, perhaps think you might hurt me?
The time has come to introduce myself.
I am called the brokenhearted one

Romantic Evening

I cannot hear you
In spite of all my efforts
I look for answers on a dead-end street
So that I might feel you
I look for your hands
So that I might touch them and feel their shape
Upon my charred body
The one you burned with your fire
The one you opened like your deck of cards
When you passed by there everyday
You slipped
You dripped and filled your heart with remorse
You passed by as if I did not live there
You opened the window and entered through it
But never through the door
As if you were afraid to touch the scarf
Of the lovely basil
And the little creek.
And now?
A harlot with obstacles
Because you did not touch me again with those hands.
Because you did not stay long and decided to leave.
Because I didn't have the time to love you.
Because you were afraid you might fall in love with me.

Woman

Wife and companion
I carried your child
Sold out girlfriend, vain lover
Harlot with a wealth of feelings at a poor man's bazaar
Ardently in love with her first teenage sweetheart
Wed to pain, to sorrow and to loneliness.
Yellow with sickness
And red with passion.
Pale from experience
And blackened from life.

When Will You Learn

That love is a harmless razor?
That on nights when you wake up alone
In uncultivated fields
And the poplars
Are glowing from a light
That you do not see
That besides, is not worth seeing.
And it is Eros that slowly fades it out
Until the next one is lit
And glows from within the wheat fields
And the poplars
From within your son's blonde hair
From within your green eyes.

I Left

I declared surrender
He said "don't do it!
You may be sorry"
I didn't listen
How could I?
It is like asking the blind to see the light
To see the colors of the flowers on
the sand
Like asking a poet to analyze the
thoughts
He wrote on his piece of paper
Like asking someone in love to see his lover's betrayal
I left
I did not look back
He called to me "Come back! Look at me! Listen to me!"
But I did not waver
From that road I had chosen
And it is one of those rough roads
That ruins your shoes.
One of those with neither seeds nor blossoms to
survive
In that way I was barren too
Barren of thoughts
Of love
Even of being weary because as it goes love makes you
weary
And rested that I was
I thought to find comfort in what he and I had in common.

12

This pessimism springs from within, they say

From the depths
But you see, I do not know how to swim
I never learned.
Others take me
By force
Those yellow leaves fall down, they say
From high up.
But don't they see how hard they try to fly?
I learned it long ago.
And they are still trying
To rid my mind of it.
Those stone hands are only for the difficulties... they say
For the difficulties...
But they fall upon the innocent hands of children and the naïve.
I learned this well
And am still trying
To forget it...

Dreams

What are dreams?
Are they those white existences in the eyes
of one who sleeps
Or the multi-colored travels of my mind?
Are they the birds that sing
Without knowing the how and the why?
Are they the children running
To catch a bit of light from life?
No
I don't know if you hear me
Or if you see how I laugh when I'm far from you
I am well...
You must know...
Only that...
And if, for no reason, you wish to see your dreams
Search well, perhaps you will find me
In them too
I will be dressed in white
Like your shadow
Like your kiss when you were going far away

Photograph

I looked for you in telephones and on screens
In a plethora of words and letters
One morning
Without knowing why
Without knowing whether you, yourself would find me
Disappointments
Joys
Life and death at once
And suddenly
I saw you.
Smiling in a photograph.
I thought it was you
You, looking at the lens
without knowing the why
That artlessness is what I loved
From the beginning
My eyes shone when they saw you
My fingers trembled when they touched you
My soul was calmed when I held you
And now my eyes are always shining
My fingers tremble
My soul is at peace
And I fear that I will lose you...

Forbidding

Do not look at me
Since you have no significant reason to exist
Do not ask me
Since you know I will not answer
Do not strike me
Since you know that I hurt and do not speak
Do not love me
Since you sense that is why I am hurting

There

There where dreams lead us
Let us go there.
There
There where the sea ends
There where the sun draws near
There where love begins
And jealousy, fear and endurance surface
Do you wonder?
Do you want to know?
Why ask the stranger?
What will he tell you?
Why should the stranger be the wise one and not you?
The soul is a stranger to you...

Empty Void

You were afraid I would leave.
That I might go far away and forget you.
But do not fear. I know how to depart...
I usually go half-way and then return.
Why?
Need you ask?
You see, it is that I live alone.
That I make coffee for myself. And not for another.
You know, it is that I live alone.
That I buy and sell precious things on my own.
That is how I bought you.
Alone one night, drinking, hurting.
You came near and whispered "what's wrong?"
You thought it enchanting that I did not speak.
You found it charming. Fateful.
And now you are speechless after so many years
When you learn that I never spoke.
That you did not hear the sound of my voice
In this empty house.
But how could you hear?
I ask you!
No one learns alone...

Passenger

Are you alive?
He asked me candidly.
Knowing I would not answer.
What could I say?
I myself did not even know if I was really alive.
After the passenger dies, it is difficult for the
vehicle to live.

Sin

Night
Dead of night and blackness
Cold
Rain falls on the black couple sitting on the bench
Snow
Two shadows huddled together
Like an image in a romantic film...
Did you come?
When? Without my hearing you?
Did you perhaps bring the gift you promised me?
You know, the one you gave me when I was a child.
No?
All right, no matter...
Anyway I have forgotten how it was...
Although I looked for it everywhere.
But it doesn't matter. Really.
You keep it.
What?
Do I want you to bring me another?
No... I wanted only that one.
To keep as absolution from sin...
What sin?
Why... That I adored you and you were my God...

Memories

Those
The white ones, the fair ones
Your colors
Those
The ones I touched again
And your kisses
The ones I used to see
In your eyes
The ones
That left once more
With your shadow

You are falling

You are falling
and the void is reminiscent of love
of youth, jasmine and bitter almonds
in a red embrace of kisses.
A child asks "what is it?"
a breath perchance?
or a cure?
Perhaps it is not love
but only a delusion that passes?
You feel empty
/in an instant
Emptiness...
You start to leave
Where will you go?
Has your love already escaped you?

I Often Wonder

*If your thoughts could fit
On a piece of white paper.
On material made by human hands.
And there are moments when your thought deceives you
When it burns whatever you left behind
When it melts like a colored candle
That leaves blotches of myriad colors
Filled with mistakes, hatred and loves
Filled with doubt and unawareness
Still in love with each other
Because they do not know what will become of them,
Lines, circles or nothing.
Still upright among us, but within the void, empty and alone.*

Joanna Kotsoni grew up in Athens. She graduated from the Varvakeion School. She studied acting and Decoration. During her study at the Drama School, she began writing poetry influenced by poems by Andreas Empeirikos. She works as an actor, while engaged in painting and continues her studies on acting and cinematography.

www.ingramcontent.com/pod-product-compliance
Lightning Source LLC
Chambersburg PA
CBHW031509040426
42444CB00007B/1274